Amazing
Tropical Birds

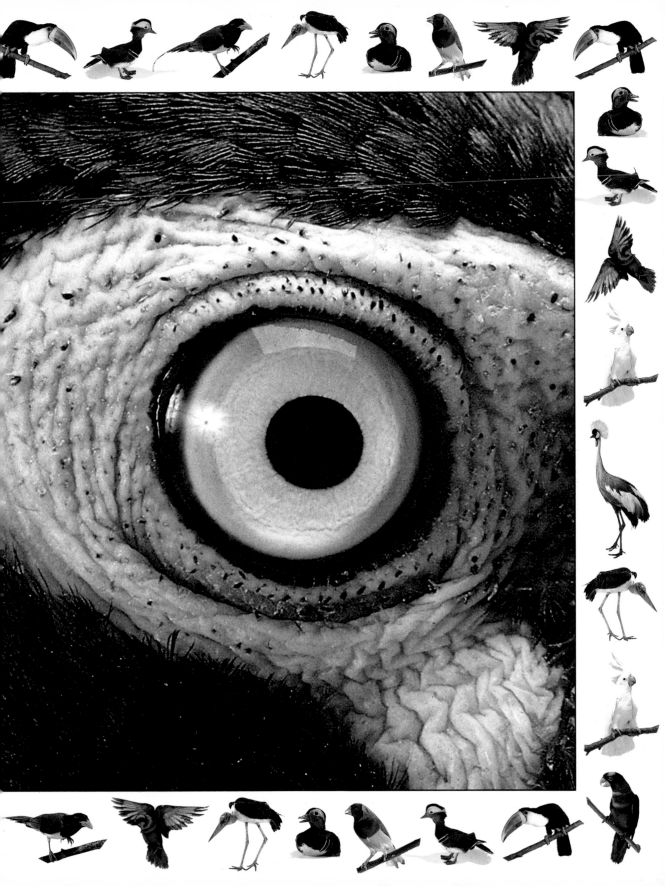

EYEWITNESS JUNIORS

Amazing Tropical Birds

WRITTEN BY
GERALD LEGG

PHOTOGRAPHED BY
JERRY YOUNG

ALFRED A. KNOPF • NEW YORK

Conceived and produced by Dorling Kindersley Limited

Project editor Christine Webb
Art editor Ann Cannings
Senior art editor Jacquie Gulliver
Senior editor Helen Parker
Production Louise Barratt

Illustrations by Mark Iley and Jane Gedye
Animals supplied by Trevor Smith's Animal World
Editorial consultants The staff of the Natural History Museum, London
Special thanks to Carl Gombrich and Kate Raworth for research,
and the Booth Museum, Brighton

Library of Congress Cataloging in Publication Data
Legg, Gerald.
Amazing tropical birds / written by Gerald Legg;
photographed by Jerry Young.
p. cm. — (Eyewitness juniors; 15)
Includes index.
Summary: Text and photographs introduce amazing tropical birds,
including the Gouldian finch, Lady Amherst's pheasant, and the
citrine-crested cockatoo.
1. Birds — Tropics — Juvenile literature. 2. Birds — Tropics —
Pictorial works — Juvenile literature. [1. Birds — Tropics.]
I. Young, Jerry, ill. II. Title. III. Series.
QL695.5.L44   1991   598.29'13 — dc20   91-6515
ISBN   0-679-81520-1
ISBN   0-679-91520-6 (lib. bdg.)

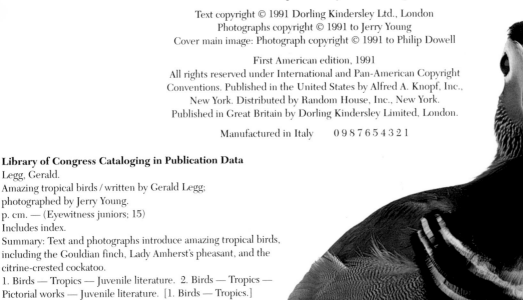

Color reproduction by Colourscan, Singapore
Printed in Italy by A. Mondadori Editore, Verona

Contents

Living in the tropics

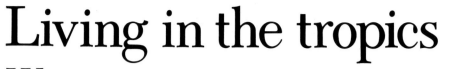

Whin it's hot and wet or hot and dry most of the year round, you know you're in the tropics. All the birds living here are called tropical birds.

Male finch

Tropical world
The strip between the tropics of Cancer and Capricorn is like a hot belt around the middle of the world. The countries in this belt are called tropical countries.

Jungle paradise
Hot tropical forests are teeming with plants and animals. Here you'll find all sorts of birds, from dull-brown ones to beautiful rainbow-bright ones, like this quetzal from Costa Rica.

Gouldian finches
These little finches are about 4 inches long. They live in small flocks on the northern Australian grasslands.

Ants to secretaries

You'll find more than half of all the kinds of birds in the world in the tropics. Some of them have unusual names, such as the antbird, the cowbird, and the secretary bird.

Dusty desert

Sandy, rocky deserts are tough places to live in. Scavenging birds, like the Egyptian vulture, help clean the land of dead animals. Because mealtimes are such gory affairs, the vulture has no feathers on its head and neck.

Water baby

The Eurasian kingfisher lives by rivers in parts of Europe and Asia. It dives in headfirst and catches fish with its sharp, pointed beak.

Female finch

Grassy savanna

Flat plains of grass and bush are home to ostriches. These huge birds cannot fly. Instead, they use their long legs to flee from trouble at speeds of up to 40 miles per hour.

Talking with color

Some birds' feathers are so colorful that they look as if they've been dipped in multicolored paint! These bright colors help them "talk" to one another, while dull colors help them hide from enemies.

Who are you?
Green-winged and scarlet macaws from South America share the same forests. They recognize the special colors and patterns of each other's feathers and know who's who in their neighborhood.

Breathing branches
The tawny frogmouth has no need for colorful feathers. It is well camouflaged at dusk, when it is hunting, and during the day, when it sleeps. Perched on a bare branch, it does its best to pretend it is part of the tree!

Watch this!
Some male birds will do anything to attract a mate. Birds of paradise put on a circus act, displaying their brilliant blue and green colors to dazzle the females.

Sitting on the nest
It is nice to be seen some of the time, but not all of the time. The female Sri Lankan jungle fowl is dull brown, so she will be as safe as possible while she sits on her eggs. Her mate is bright and flashy.

Female

Male

Fancy feathers

What makes some feathers dull gray and others bright blue? Pigments, or "dyes," in feathers give them their color. They are just like the pigments that make grass green and blood red.

Shimmering colors

Some feathers shimmer and change color when you tilt them. Like the rainbows you can see on soap bubbles, these colors appear when sunlight falls on them.

This male pheasant measures nearly 3 feet from head to tail

Go away!

Male birds don't use their flashy colors just to attract a mate. The hawk-headed parrot fluffs up the feathers on its head and neck to warn off enemies, too.

Lady Amherst's pheasant

For a long time, people in the West thought that this Chinese pheasant was not real because it was so beautiful.

A bird's-eye view

Wouldn't you like to be able to fly like a bird? Just imagine – you could swoop, glide, dive, and soar across the oceans and mountains, and have a bird's-eye view of what's going on below.

This lorikeet is 7 inches long. Fully grown lorikeets may be 16 inches long.

Winter holiday

White storks have the best of both worlds. They spend the warm summer in Europe. In winter, they travel 4,000 miles south to tropical Africa.

Underwater paddles

The brown pelican from Central America is a water baby. It plunges into the sea with a flap of its wings and dives underwater. Pushing with its webbed feet, it races after its favorite fish supper.

High flier

In a Greek legend, Icarus and his father were trapped in a maze. They escaped by flying out with wings made of wax and feathers. But Icarus flew too close to the sun. The wax melted, and he fell into the sea.

Helicopter hover

Hummingbirds perform amazing tricks in the air as they search for and sip nectar from flowers. They dart up, down, sideways, backward – and they can even keep stock-still in midair.

Shady view

The long-legged black heron of Africa has a clever use for its wings. It holds them out over the water, making shade for the fish. If a fish swims into the shade, the heron snaps it up.

It's quicker by air

Rainbow lorikeets fly around in flocks, looking for gum trees, which are full of nectar and pollen.

Expert glider

Once the sooty tern has left home, it may not land, or settle on water, until nesting time – 3 or 4 years later!

All-purpose tools

Birds do not have hands, so their beaks and feet have to do all the work. These tools are tailor-made for the job at hand – or claw!

Nut crackers

The strong, short beak of the scarlet macaw can crack open a tough nut as easily as biting into a soft banana. The macaw uses its feet like hands to hold food while it is eating.

Walking on water

The lily trotter has incredibly long toes. They help the bird tiptoe over floating lily pads in its watery Australian home – without sinking.

Fruit pickers

The toco toucan's enormous beak is a useful tool for picking fruit and berries way out on the tips of branches, where they're hard to reach.

Sacred ibis

The long, curved beak of the ibis makes catching slippery prey seem easy work. In ancient Egypt, the sacred ibis was the symbol of the moon god, Thoth, because its beak looked like the crescent moon.

Scrunchy insects

A strong, but not too large, beak is ideal for catching and crunching grasshoppers and beetles. The Indian roller (right) sits on a post, ready to swoop down on its prey.

Nectar sippers
The malachite sunbird uses its long beak and tongue to probe into flowers and reach the nectar inside. First it finds a perch near the flowers. Then it digs into a nectar feast.

Seed peckers
Vermilion cardinals are seed eaters. They have to break open the hard shell to get to the tasty seed inside. Short, stout beaks and strong jaws make the job easier.

This roller's body is nearly 10 inches long

Meat eaters
African fish eagles have short, curved beaks for tearing flesh. Sharp claws, or talons, on powerful feet grip the prey – and can even kill it.

Help from friends

Many birds help each other, and some even help other animals too. It's great to have a friendly beak or pair of feet when you're in a tight spot!

In line . . . march!

Secretary birds strut side by side on the grasslands of Africa. If they spot a snake, they kick it and stomp on it. To protect them from snake bites, their amazingly long legs are covered with tough scales.

Hitchhiking

The Arabian bustard has a broad back – just right for the carmine bee-eater to hitch a ride on. This way, the bee-eater can keep an eye out for insects disturbed by the bustard as it walks.

Safety in numbers

Many animals are safer when they stay in large groups. That's why you see schools of fish, herds of zebra, and flocks of birds as they feed and roost. In Australia, flocks of rainbow lorikeets perch in trees to eat the blossoms and drink nectar.

Watch the hooves!

Flocks of cattle egrets feed among the cattle and game on the African plains. They perch on the animals' backs, watching and waiting for the cattle to disturb insects with their feet. Then, quick as a flash, the egrets swoop down and peck up the insects.

This whydah's tail is the same length as its body – about 5 inches long

Friend or foe?

Some cuckoos lay their eggs in other birds' nests. When the cuckoo chick has hatched out, it carefully dumps all the other eggs out of the nest. This way, it gets all the attention – and all the food!

What a honey!

In parts of Africa, the greater honeyguide leads hunters to the hives of wild bees. The hunters believe that unless they give the bird some honey as a reward, the next time the bird will lead them to lions instead!

A bit to the left . . .

The red-billed oxpecker has an important job. It works as a cleaner for cattle and game. It scampers all over their backs, pecking blood-sucking ticks from the animals' skin with its small, sharp beak.

Fisher's whydah

The Fisher's whydah moves in large flocks in its African home. This keeps the flock safe – and makes food hunting easier.

Tail feathers look like straws

King of cranes

With its long, elegant body and a "crown" of feathers on its head, the crowned crane is the king of all cranes.

Flying high

When cranes fly, they stick their long necks straight out in front of them and flap away.

Eurasian crane

Tropical cranes

There are many kinds of tropical crane. Australian cranes live in Australia, Sarus cranes live in India, and Eurasian cranes spend winters in Africa and Asia.

Sarus crane

Australian crane

Lookout

Long legs and a long neck give the crowned crane a good view all around. This way, it can easily spot insects and frogs which it disturbs with its feet as it moves around.

Song and dance

When they're courting, crane couples like to dance. First they bob up and down. Then they leap toward each other, flapping their wings. They circle each other, leap apart, then leap toward each other. Try doing that in a rush!

All together now

Crane couples sing together when they are courting. They stand side by side, with their wings folded and their necks stretched upward. Then they make loud honking noises.

All cranes go to heaven

The Chinese believe that cranes are symbols of long life. Ancient Chinese thought that when people died, their souls rode to heaven on a crane's back.

Crowned crane
Special, strawlike feathers form the "crown" of the black crowned crane.

This crane stands about 3 feet high

19

Sounds amazing

When you're walking in a tropical forest, don't worry if you hear tweets, croaks, screams, and chatters drifting down through the trees. It's the birds' way of letting everyone know they're around.

What a laugh!
If you're ever camping in the Australian bush, you won't need an alarm clock. The laughing kookaburra gives a loud, cackling early-morning call that's sure to get you up in a hurry!

Weird sounds
Some birds can't make up their minds what they want to be. Bowerbirds have been heard imitating cats, dogs, car horns, axes chopping wood, and fence wires twanging!

Turn up the volume!
Some bird calls can be heard more than a mile away. The rhinoceros hornbill uses the "box" on top of its enormous beak to make its call louder, so it will travel through the thick Malaysian jungle.

Look out!
Never pick a fight with a common turkey. If it's disturbed, it fluffs its feathers up and gobbles and clucks to frighten off enemies. Then it attacks, using its powerful wings, feet, and beak.

Citrine-crested cockatoos are only found on Sumba Island, in Indonesia

Male citrine-crested cockatoos like this one have dark-brown eyes, while females have brownish-red eyes

Sing me a song!

People have kept pet birds for a very long time. Some like to hear the beautiful songs of canaries; others train their parrots or parakeets to imitate human speech!

Perfectly tuned

When a pair of D'Arnaud's barbets meet, the two birds often break into a duet. Their voices are so perfectly tuned that it sounds as if only one of them is singing.

Chatterbox

As they fly, large flocks of citrine-crested cockatoos keep in touch with loud, harsh screeches and squawks.

This cockatoo measures over 9 inches from head to tail

Weird and wonderful

Some tropical birds would certainly stand out in a crowd. Weird beaks and wings – and strange little habits – all help to make these birds seem very peculiar.

A bird that climbs?
The hoatzin chick has a strange claw on each wing. It uses these claws to clamber around in the branches near its waterside nest. Once the chick grows up, the claws fall off.

Charge!
The cassowary can put up quite a fight if it has to. It will jump at its enemies, feet first, and knock them to the ground. Otherwise, it just lowers its head and runs for cover, using its tough "helmet" to protect its head.

Knock, knock!
Red-billed hornbills don't take any risks when they set up house. Once they've found the right tree hole, the female seals herself in, leaving a tiny hole for her mate to feed her through. She doesn't come out until her chicks are half grown.

Using a hammer
When they want a tasty ostrich egg snack, Egyptian vultures don't waste any time. They have learned to pick up stones and toss them at the egg's tough shell until it cracks open.

When it's standing straight, the marabou stork is just over 4 feet tall

Somebody loves him

The marabou stork from Africa is not a pretty sight. It uses its huge, powerful beak to pick meat from dead animals. And it doesn't mind poking around in garbage dumps for snacks, either.

Slurp, slurp!

The African spoonbill sweeps its spoon-shaped beak from side to side in the water. Any passing fish are snapped up by the spoon. A quick jerk of the head, and down the hatch they go!

You can't wear this shoe

The odd beak of the African shoebill looks a little like an oversize shoe. But it is just the right size for catching fish, water snakes, and frogs – and for carrying water to thirsty chicks.

In the rain forest

The dark, damp world of the rain forest is teeming with fruit, flowers, and insects. That's why you'll find birds searching for food on the ground, in the branches, and even high up in the treetops – all year round.

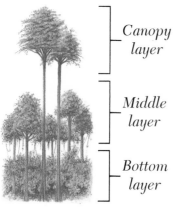

Canopy layer

Middle layer

Bottom layer

Upstairs, downstairs
Each bird has its home in a particular layer of the rain forest. Some live on the dark forest floor, some live in the branches of shorter trees, and others live right at the top, in the canopy.

This toucan measures 18 inches from the tip of its tail to the tip of its beak

Above the trees
Next time you're flying over a rain forest, keep an eye out for this Cuvier's toucan. It lives in the canopy and uses its long, strong beak to reach fruit at the very ends of branches.

The Cuvier's toucan throws its head back and tosses fruit down its throat

On the floor

The rain forest is so thick and tall that it is very dark on the forest floor. This is where the blue-breasted pitta lives, scratching about for snails, insects, fallen fruit, and seeds.

Branching out

In the thick of the rain forest, between the floor and the canopy, the blue-crowned motmot darts from branch to branch, snapping up insects in its sharp beak.

Monkeys too

The monkey-eating eagle soars over the forest canopy in search of its favorite meal – monkey! It doesn't mind the occasional hornbill or piglet, either.

God of the air

The quetzal was worshiped by Aztec Indians. Only the Aztec royal family could wear its long tail feathers – and they had to be plucked without killing the bird!

What rain forest?

The tropics used to be covered with rain forests. Now only half of them remain. Every time a tree is cut down, the birds and other animals that live in it lose their homes.

To find a mate

Male birds have to have all their wits about them when they're looking for a mate. Sometimes, being colorful isn't enough. They have to be good dancers and singers, too!

What a lovely fan!
Once he spots a female, the Victoria riflebird spreads his wings like a fan, with the tips almost touching. If the show is good enough, the birds will mate and rear a family.

A song and dance
The New Guinean magnificent bird of paradise has an amazing dance routine. He sidles up and down on a twig, flashing his green breast feathers and blue feet.

Tunnel of love
The male satin bowerbird builds a "bower," or tunnel of grass, on the ground, and entices his mate into it. He decorates his bower with any blue object he can find – even clothespins and berries!

May I have this dance?
When it's courting, the blue-footed booby breaks into a tap-dance routine, showing off his bright blue feet.

Look at me!
The male mandarin duck swims around his dull mate to impress her. This way, he can show off his feathers to their best advantage.

Showing off
Early in the breeding season, male mandarin ducks are smartly dressed in their brilliant feathers.

Flashy party
The Guianan cock-of-the-rock gets together with his male friends. They show off to the local females with their fine feathers and song, hoping to find a partner.

This mandarin duck is 17 inches long

All puffed up
The frigatebird has an unusual way of attracting a mate. He perches in a tree and tries to impress females flying overhead by inflating a brilliant red pouch on his throat.

Homes for the chicks

Birds build nests with all sorts of things and in all kinds of places. But however the nests are made, they must be safe and warm for the eggs and chicks.

Tiniest nest
The bee hummingbird is the smallest bird in the world. It measures about 2 inches from the tip of its beak to the tip of its tail. Its tiny nest could sit on a quarter!

This magpie's body is 28 inches long

The blue magpie lives in parts of Southeast Asia

Tangle of twigs
To hide its eggs and chicks from unwelcome visitors, the blue magpie builds a large nest of tangled twigs deep within the branches of shrubs and bushes.

Twiglets

The fairy tern balances its egg on the fork of small branches. How the egg manages to stay there is quite amazing!

The magpie's tail has black-and-white bands on the underside

Meal of a nest

In Southeast Asia, bird's-nest soup is a delicacy. You won't find a bunch of twigs floating in your soup, though – the nests are made from the saliva of birds called swiftlets.

Open sesame!

The Cape penduline tit is a clever bird. It builds a big false entrance for its nest. The false entrance distracts snakes and other enemies from the real entrance, hidden nearby.

Real entrance

False entrance

Woven basket

Male weaverbirds weave and knot grass stalks to make their nests, which dangle from the end of twigs. The better this male's nest looks, the more chance he has to attract a mate.

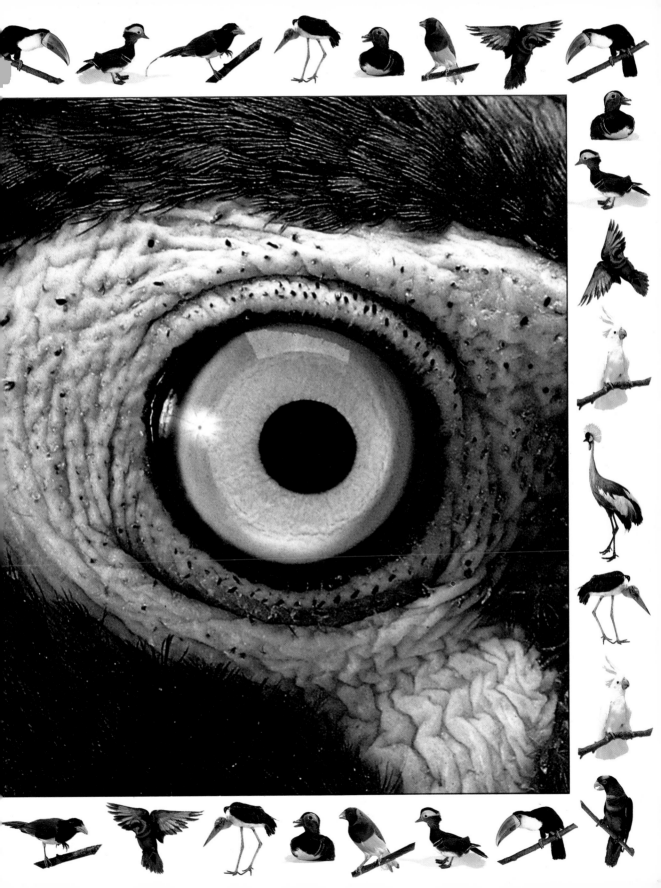